DATING FOR WOMEN PLAYBOOK

Transformational Dating Advice For Women Including How To Achieve Better Relationships, Effortlessly Attract More Men, Online Dating Tips & Tinder Secrets To Boost Your Self-Esteem

By Matthew Stone & Julie Hussey

© 2018

©Copyright 2018 – All rights reserved

The contents of this book may not be reproduced, duplicated or transmitted without direct written permission from the author.

Under no circumstances will any legal responsibility or blame be held against the author or publisher for any reparation, damage or monetary loss due to the information herein, either directly or indirectly.

Legal Notice

This book is copyright protected. This is for personal use only. You cannot amend, distribute, sell, use, quote or paraphrase any part of the content in this book without written consent from the author.

Disclaimer Notice

Please note that the information contained within this document is for educational and entertainment purposes only. Every attempt has been made to provide accurate, up to date and reliable information. No warranties of any kind are expressed or implied. Readers acknowledge that the author is not engaging the rendering of legal, financial, medical or professional advice. The content of this book has been derived from various sources. Please consult a licensed professional before attempting any techniques outlined in this book.

By reading this document, the reader agrees that under no circumstance is the author responsible for any losses, direct or indirect, that are incurred as a result of the use of the information contained within this document, including – but not limited to – errors, omissions or inaccuracies.

Table of Contents

Introduction 1

Chapter 1: Using Your Emotions as A Tool 6

Chapter 2: Confidence Is Key 23

Chapter 3: Finding the Right Partner 36

Chapter 4: Attracting Other People 48

Chapter 5: Navigating Online Dating 59

Chapter 6: Some Dating Tips You'll Actually Use 73

Chapter 7: Maintaining the Relationship You Worked For 86

Chapter 8: Applying All This to Real Life 98

Chapter 9: Having Fun with It All 103

Conclusion 105

Introduction

The goal after reading this book is for women to feel intensely empowered. This can be done once your perspective on the dating world and men in general changes. Once the secrets of dating have been uncovered and learned by you as the reader, your life will completely change. It won't be long before men are knocking at your door, begging to date you. Not only will the dates increase, but the ability to maintain positive and healthy relationships with your suitors will become stronger as well. If you're ready to find your Mr. Right, have him fall hard for you, and spend the rest of your life living out your dream, this is the place to start!

It all begins with changing your perception on dating as a whole. It doesn't matter if you're freshly single from a long marriage or a committed relationship. Maybe you've never dated in your life and are ready to start. Perhaps you've been trying to find the right one for an endless amount of time with no luck. Women of all shapes, sizes, colours, and everything in between can find their happily ever after by starting off with this book. It's all already inside of you, and we're here to help make sure you find what it takes to fulfil your dating fantasies.

When you see couples that seem mismatched, or a partner that seems unattractive, you might wonder what it is about the two that made them fall for each other. There are some women that seem to have every man in the world vying for their attention, and others that seem to have it all, but no men have any interest in them. It might make you wonder, what is it about these women that the other women are lacking?

It comes natural to some women, and others need to practice and study to become the most desirable. It starts with the manipulation of the male mind, and once this technique is mastered, it can feel like a superpower.

In this book, we're going to break down for you what these powers are and how you can take them and apply them to your everyday life. Not every woman will learn of these powers and figure out how to use them. They might still get dates and have relationships, but in the end, they might be more likely to face heartbreak.

It can be easy to become a bitter woman, broken down by men and heartbreak. Maybe there's one guy that you just can't seem to get out of your head. He might hurt you, but there's something about him that keeps you coming back. Maybe there was just one guy that messed everything up and made it difficult for you to open yourself up and love again. There are plenty of men that are cheaters, liars, and overall douchebags.

Surprisingly, we believe that not all men are like this. It can be hard to come to terms with that, but in reality, there are plenty of amazing men out there that are ready to make you theirs! It's not about luck, chance, or just finding the right man waiting for you on your doorstep. The key is understanding what makes a good man and being able to pick them out of a crowd. More importantly is being the type of woman that that good man wants to be faithful and dedicated to. This is the challenging part, but the powers we go over in the book will help you get there.

The more you know, the more powerful you can become. This is what you've been waiting for, and everything is about to change. Instead of getting your heart broken, you're the one that's going to be doing the breaking. It can be scary to risk it all, but in the end, it might be the most exciting thing you'll ever do.

We've broken the book into nine parts for you. In each of these parts, we're going to discuss the essential ideas necessary to achieve your dating goals. Think of it like a 'Dating Playbook' It's encouraged to take notes throughout the book, so you can see some examples, arguments, and other helpful tips that you can apply to your everyday life. Revisiting these ideas will only help grow your knowledge, which, in turn, will grow your power.

Just a warning before you get into the book, it might not be for everyone. There are going to be moments of brutal honesty, bluntness, and other things that aren't easy to hear. It might be scary but confronting these challenges will only make you stronger in the end.

This isn't about being delicate, because that's not what's in store for you in the dating world. It's time to be realistic with yourself and the world, but that doesn't have to be a bad thing. You just have to be willing to confront yourself. You're going to have to dig deep inside your mind, soul, and body. If you stay committed to this book and your dreams of a better dating life, it will happen for you. Most importantly, you have to be ready for a change. A big one.

There's a reason why you're reading this book. You've already come into this with a predisposed image on men and dating. That has to change. Don't worry, you won't be doing it all on your own. We're here to help. We can't do everything, however. You have to be the one that's willing to jump in the deep end, no matter how cold the water might be.

It can be uncomfortable to apply these ideas to your real life, but that's what it's all about.

Normal isn't comfortable, and your normal hasn't been working thus far, so it's time to change things up. It's time to be brave, willing to change, and ready for the future. It'll take practice, but everything does. Nothing's going to happen overnight. You're not going to finish the book and instantly get a text or knock on your door from a man. It's not easy, but this book will give you all the tools you need to find the person you've been looking for.

The first step, even before starting the first chapter, is to open yourself up. Leave behind all the other ideas you've had about men and dating and start fresh today. The experiences you've had are certainly important, but don't let them define you anymore. Once you're able to do that and take the tools we give you in this book, you'll be able to find The One, and never let another man make you hurt.

So, without further ado, let's get started!

Chapter 1: Using Your Emotions as A Tool

Emotions come naturally to us, so of course, it's going to be challenging to learn to use and manipulate your own feelings to your advantage. That's why we put this chapter first. If you can conquer your own emotions, you'll be able to breeze through the rest of the book with ease.

Women are known for being the more emotional of the sexes, men being the more sexually driven. That's why it can be so challenging to control your emotions. We're wired to listen to them. They're ingrained in our bodies for protection and healing. Men have them too, but in the dating world, it seems their sexual desire takes rank. It doesn't matter where you're from, this will likely remain true. We all look different and act opposite on the outside, but on the inside, we have the same innerworkings, the same wires that are biologically placed.

Don't deny your own natural instincts. It's not about turning off your emotions. If you did that, you wouldn't be human anymore. Our ability to think and feel so deeply is a tool that allows us to be great mothers, lovers, sisters, and friends.

Get the idea that emotional equals weak out of your head ASAP. Everyone has emotions, and women just happen to feel them a bit more. This by no means proves that women are weak in any way. They are actually stronger because of them, but our patriarchal society would have you feeling otherwise. We're not asking you to lose all emotion. Just learn how to control them and use them to your advantage rather than allowing them to be your weakness.

Once you gain power over your emotions, you'll also gain power over men. Men have been using our emotions against us for far too long. They call you weak, whiny, moody, and anything else they can to make you feel as though your emotions are wrong. These words are meant to hurt you, but you should allow them to make you feel more powerful.

It's time for a new normal. We can easily let ourselves fall into relationships that are unhealthy just because it's normal. Maybe you saw your mother or friend in a bad relationship, and now you're in one yourself, all because it's what seems normal. Normal isn't always right, and we're here to help you really flip the switch and take back charge of your emotions.

Men Are Already in Control of Your Emotions

You're reading this because you want to figure men out. What you need to know, is that there are some men already have a pretty decent grasp on our emotions. Men have been manipulating us, lying and cheating for centuries. That's because they're able to logically look at our emotions and use them as our weaknesses.

Some men don't even realize what they're doing. Women make it too easy for men and allow them to take a part of themselves and turn it around, only to have it used against them. There are still plenty of men that know exactly what they're doing, and these are the most dangerous kinds. It's best to just avoid these men, but, if you do run into one, we hope you'll have the tools to take control.

While there are plenty of Prince Charming's in the world, there are still plenty of men that can be dangerous when it comes to using your own emotions against you. They can manipulate your feelings to exactly what they want, which includes money, sex, or maybe just a place to stay. Men are good at this, but it's time for women to be even better.

Of course, not all men are like this. When we talk about men, we're speaking on the general population, but it's important for you to not look at every single man as someone you should conquer. That doesn't mean you can't be prepared should you come face to face with someone that might try to manipulate you.

Some men, or people in general, will use you up and take everything you have, but only if you let them. They'll take every part of you to get what you want, so when they leave, of course you're going to follow! They took who you were and changed it into someone that they wanted, someone they could use. Once they're done and have had their way, you feel lost and lonely. Before it gets to this point, you have to control your emotions, so they never get to take a piece of you in the first place.

We've become bullseyes because of our own emotions. We do some silly and stupid things sometimes all in the name of our emotions. We all have that person in our past that we think about now and wonder how it lasted as long as it did. How often do you see someone you dated, wishing so badly you hadn't given them a part of you? Our emotions can cause us to do silly things, but they can also make us incredibly powerful.

Differentiate listening to your heart and head. This is one of the most important steps in controlling your emotions. We've heard it all the time, but it's true! Your heart is telling you what it thinks you want to hear. It's easy to follow your heart. Listen to your head!

Let's think of this in a logical scenario. We all know that one guy, whether you dated them, or a friend did, that was just an absolutely terrible partner. Maybe he was selfish, a slob, or a lying cheat. Either way, there's something about him that just makes him awful, but he still ended up taking control of your or your friend's heart.

Once the relationship ended, it's very clear to see that logically, you should never ever go back to that man. When it comes to your heart, however, it's going to tell you to run right back to him. This is because our hearts are hurting. They're doing what they think is right to mend the problem. You're going to run back into his arms and it'll feel great! But only for a moment. Our brain knows what's best. It's going to hurt, but you have to do what's right and just walk away.

The Emotional End of a Relationship

One of the hardest things you'll have to face when entering the dating world is accepting the end of a relationship. Breakups are hard, and no one is going to argue with that. Some of us might find the right one on our first date, and others go through more breakups than an entire group of women combined. Either way, breaking up is going to be hard to do.

You might want to follow your emotions in an attempt to feel better, but you have to look at this logically. Like we already discussed, your heart is used to something normal. When your heart feels pain, its biological response is to make the pain go away. It seems as though going back to the norm is what's going to fix everything, but we have to resist that urge.

Your emotions can make you stupid. How many girls do you know that were so desperate to get back with someone they did something completely crazy? There are going to be emotions at the end of a relationship, and you might have the urge to do things you would never do otherwise. Just remind yourself that this is your heart speaking. We're going to teach you how to better listen to your head.

Identifying and Governing Your Responses

Actually, recognizing your emotions can be rather easy. It can be simple to know if you're sad, depressed, hopeless, or whatever other emotion you might be feeling. It's common for people to be sad after a breakup. Perhaps you might even feel a little relief. Along with the sadness of what was lost, you're going to feel anxiety as well. Did I make the right choice? Did I just mess everything up? That's our brain's natural reaction, and that's completely fine.

The hard part is determining how to control your reaction. The emotions aren't the problem. It's what you do with those emotions that can really make things go sour. You're going to be sad, and you're going to want to call him after a breakup. Being sad isn't wrong! But calling him is! It's important to know that you're not at fault for feeling bad, but you are for being weak and picking up the phone even though you know you shouldn't.

You have to be strong. This is where the willpower really comes in. Patience is the most important part of a breakup. If you broke your leg, you wouldn't expect to go running the next day, right? Try and treat your heart the same way.

Accepting is another challenging part. You must accept that you are going to feel pain. You are going to hurt. Unfortunately, there's just no way to avoid this. You're human! If you learn how to handle this pain, however, instead of allowing that hurt to keep you glued to your bed, you can learn how to use it as a tool to thrive.

Mending Your Broken Heart

Distraction is one of the greatest tools when it comes to fixing what was broken. If only we could just use some scotch tape or glue to help us feel better when we've fallen apart. Our hearts and brains don't work that way. Instead, distraction is a key part in moving on.

You're going to think about him. There's no eraser for memories or way to block out certain thoughts. Even if there were, that's not the healthy way to handle things! When you're with friends, maybe you hear a song that reminds you of him. Maybe he was so important in your life that even the sidewalk you're stepping on causes you to think of him! This is normal, but don't let it control you. Don't let your emotions do something that you'll regret.

It's going to be painful, but distraction will help. The more you can keep your mind off of your ex, the easier it will be to move on. If you don't let your mind wander to the dark corners of your brain, you won't be asking yourself those anxiety-inducing questions such as, does he still love me? Did I do the right thing?

The pain will dissolve. It might never go away, just like a broken bone will never heal the exact way it was in the beginning. This doesn't mean your leg isn't good anymore! It's just different now, but in a way, it can be even stronger!

A Quick Guide for Controlling Emotions

1. Emotions are natural. Remember that you are not at fault for the way you feel. It's OK to be sad, angry, and emotional.
2. Don't let your emotions dictate. It's perfectly fine to feel the way you feel, but

the key is how you let your feelings control your actions.
3. Accept that you will feel pain. This is inevitable. You can't have the good without the bad first, but trust me, the good will be worth it in the end.
4. You are in control! It might feel like you're falling down a hole with no grip but remember that it's your mind. Your heart. Your brain. You're in charge, even in the times you don't feel that way.
5. Let yourself heal. Don't put yourself down because you're still thinking of him. Don't force yourself into more painful situations. It's time to heal, and that's OK.
6. Distraction is key! The more you keep your mind occupied, the less of a chance that it'll trick you into doing something stupid and based on your emotions and anxieties.

Don't Give the Man Anymore Power

You're going to want to check his social media. You might even drive or walk by where he works or lives. This is normal. Everyone has the desire to see what's going on with the person that took a piece of you. Those are your emotions. Your emotional state will make you want to do those silly things. Now it's time to control them. You're in charge. You decide if you're actually going to do that.

The pain will be there but direct it towards something else! It's normal to want to become a private investigator of your ex after things have ended. It's going to hurt, and you might think that seeing what they're up to will help make you feel better. It might, but just for a moment. Stay strong, patient, and accepting. Understand that it's going to take time, and don't let that man take anymore of your time than you've already given him.

The Greatest Distractions to Mend Your Heart

As we've already discussed, you're going to need to distract yourself. When a baby's crying, the first thing a mom might do is distract it with something shiny. Eventually, the baby forgets why it was crying in the first place! It might seem silly, but the same can be said about our emotions! We were all babies at one point, after all. We're going to share with you some distractions that'll help mend your broken heart.

Practice Dates

Dating is the best way to start the healing process. It seems counterintuitive. Remember, though, when you're hungover, sometimes the best cure is to have a drink of the same thing that made you sick in the first place! The last thing you're going to want to do is date again but getting out there and meeting new people is the best way to do it. Don't be afraid to ask for help! Maybe your friends know someone they can at least set you up with for a blind date.

You're going to think about your ex. In some cases, probably more than you think about the person sitting across from you. It's going to be hard the first, second, or third date. But eventually, you'll get back to your old self and realize the importance of meeting new people.

You don't have to commit yourself to every date. If you're on dating apps, which obviously you should be at this point, you probably get messages or at least see people you would never think to date. Why not try to use them as your practice dates? Who knows, maybe this person you never saw yourself with could actually be the one! And if they're not, at least you can't say you didn't at least try. Sometimes, when you have nothing to lose is when you gain the most.

The worst thing that could happen is that you have a boring time. That's OK! You never have to go out with them again! At least you can get a free meal from it, or maybe a funny story to share with friends later that night. It can feel wrong, knowing that you might not be fully committed to this person, but it's just a first date. How do you know that they're not doing the same thing?

Trust me, the men won't walk away being hurt. Half of them are just hoping to get into a bed for the night, but you don't have to worry about that. It's not your responsibility to make sure that the men are getting what they want. This is your turn, your time. Go out and have fun. There's no pressure for commitment, and in the end, you might make a new friend. The most important thing is to just keep yourself distracted.

Men have used women for so long, it's our turn now. Use these dates to figure out what you do and don't want. Build your confidence and realize you have what it takes to be that flirty and bubbly girl you've always envied. Now's your chance to practice conversations and see what works and what doesn't. It'll be scary at first, but in the end, so worth it.

Practice dates are one of the most important tools you'll have. It's not only a distraction, but one step further to taking power over your life.

Write A Letter to Your Ex

We know, we know. Up until this point, we've told you to cut off all contact with your ex. Now we're asking you to write a letter? Well, whatever you choose to write isn't meant for them to read, only you. Grab a pen and piece of paper and write down everything you don't like about them. Write down the things they did or said to make you mad and sad. Write down even the small stuff, like their breath smelled or their nose was too big. Nothing is off limits.

Writing down everything you loathed about the other person is your chance to really reclaim yourself. Once you're done with the letter or list, it's time for you to decide what to do. Maybe you could rip it up and throw it into the lake. Perhaps you could set it on fire with all the other things that remind you of your ex. Some might choose to keep the letter around as a reminder when they're missing the person they wrote the letter about.

These tools will help anyone and everyone who's in the dating world. It's a distraction for you and a reminder of everything wrong with that relationship. When we're separated from that, it can be easy to only remember the good things. There's a reason it didn't work out in the first place, and your letter will help remind you of that.

Your Emotions as A Weapon in The Beginning

So far, we've discussed the importance of controlling your emotions after a breakup. The struggle doesn't stop there. It's important to take control of your emotions again once you've started dating again as well. Just as easily as your emotions could make you do something silly after a breakup, they could do some damage in the beginning as well.

When you meet someone you really like, of course, you're going to want to call and text them immediately. Don't! Use that same willpower you used in your last breakup now. Put down the phone and let them come to you. Of course, you don't want to completely ignore them, but there's a fine line between being desperate and being cold. You have to find that balance, and it starts with self-control.

The Most Important Reasons to Practice Self Control

1. If you confuse him, he'll only work harder. Men don't like feeling powerless. If you're desperate and needy right away, they know they have all the power. Keep yourself cool and collected, and he'll come to you. You'll leave him confused and wondering if he likes you rather than the other way around.
2. Men are natural hunters. They like a challenge and they want what they can't have. Men like it even more if you don't seem interested, as it's a challenge they can overcome. Of course, not all men are like this, but if you go into a relationship

knowing the man is going to want a challenge, you'll end up coming out on top.
3. Rushing can cause more breakage. Your heart is fragile. You wouldn't just going throwing it around if you could hold it, would you? Take things slow so as to not allow yourself to become a victim of a broken heart again. Remember, don't get too cold, but if you practice self-control, reasons 1 and 2 come naturally to you.

How Can I Tell If He Likes Me?

Does he like me? That question can be the most stressful one you'll ask, but it can also be rather exciting. All men are different, but at the core, they share a lot of similarities. If he likes you, he's going to make it work.

Don't let yourself be the pursuer. He might be shy, but if he really likes you, if he really can't get you out of his head, he's still going to be the one to make the first move. If he doesn't put in the effort to get your attention in the first place, it's a warning sign of how much effort he'd put into the relationship.

Patience is the most important. When guys get flirty, you're instantly going to think they like you. Don't give in right away. Make him work for it!

Don't be afraid to flirt! Yes, some think it's better to wait for men to come to you, but there might be some that take a little more reassurance before they make a move. If you're flirty, this is a way to let him know that you're there and ready for some dedication. At the very least, flirting is always good practice.

If it never happens, maybe it's meant to be. Maybe he's been hurt, or maybe he's too shy to make a move. If he really likes, and really sees what makes you special, he'll work hard to get your attention. If not, there are plenty of other guys out there willing to put the work in.

Learn to take a hint. Sometimes, you just have to accept that he's not the one. It can be hard, especially if you've already invested time. Unfortunately, you have to use that patience and acceptance we've discussed to know when it's time to move onto the next.

STAY STRONG!

We've covered a lot so far, and you might start to feel a little overwhelmed. If you do, that's great! Like we said, this isn't going to be easy. You should feel a little overloaded, but don't worry, we're not done yet. This isn't easy but finding The One will be the greatest thing you'll ever do.

The most important thing for you to do is to take charge. You're in control! Emotions are not easy. Everyone has them, and everyone uses them in different ways. It's important that you use yours for empowerment, and don't let others see them as a weakness.

The same weapons used against you for so long are now yours to reclaim.

Chapter 2: Confidence Is Key

Once you achieve a high level of confidence, you can easily become indestructible. Sometimes, others see confidence as a negative quality. We often call people with high levels of confidence self-centred, or "cocky." Perhaps some feel jealous or threatened by someone else's confidence, but you can't let this scare you away from being your best self. Once you achieve high self-esteem and higher confidence, you'll feel as though nothing can break your spirit. Sticks and stones may break your bones, but words will never hurt, right?

We've been told for so long and so often to not let what others say or do bring you down. We can all agree that's way easier said than done. Let's face it: it hurts when someone says or does something mean. Even if they weren't intentionally trying to hurt us, all too often we feel bad about ourselves because of something someone else might have said or done.

It's also important to constantly challenge your thoughts. When you look in the mirror and think, "why does my face look like that?" ask yourself immediately after where you originally heard those thoughts. Did someone used to make fun of you as a child? Maybe a parent or a sibling was a little too hard on you as you grew up? Sometimes, our negative thoughts don't come from anywhere else other than our own minds. Next time you say something mean to yourself, ask afterwards, where did I get that idea? Not everything you say to yourself is true! You can have all the tools necessary to make yourself feel better, and sometimes, nothing seems to work. We're going to discuss some ideas and tips to try and help you gain the most confidence possible.

You Don't *Need* A Partner

Before entering a relationship with anyone, you have to realize that you're doing so as a way to improve your life, not complete it. You should have the capabilities to go through your day to day life on your own, without needing anyone else's help. Yes, it's way easier to do simple things when you have a partner, but you need to remind yourself you don't *need* one. It's way easier to prepare dinner, pay for things, and especially raise children with someone else. A partner can take half the work load. That doesn't mean you can't do it alone. You're a strong independent woman that doesn't need a man to survive! You have to get to a point where you want one. Instead of something you need, they become someone you want to have around. Not only can that improve your relationship, but it can change your perspective on a lot more than just your romantic life.

A partner is a lot like milk with cereal. Cereal is great on its own, just snacking on the small pieces. But once you add the milk, it gets a whole lot better. Understand that you're still a valuable person without a partner. You don't need a man, you *want* one. Once you start accepting that truth, you'll realize different qualities in a partner that you didn't know you wanted. A romantic partner should be one that compliments you, not completes you. The thought of finding someone that you love so much you can't live without is a romantic and grandiose idea. It's not realistic, however. That kind of love can be painful and dangerous.

This also allows you to leave an unhealthy relationship should you find yourself in one. You should never find yourself in a position with a partner that you don't want to be with, only because you're scared that you might not make it without them. There have been plenty of stories of women staying with partners they didn't love only because they offered financial support. There are just as many cases of women dating men only because they're wealthy. Having financial support is amazing, but not as much as true love. Them having money should be a benefit, not a necessity.

The only person you should be depending on is you. You'll go through life much easier if you accept that you're the only one in charge of your happiness. Only you can control how you feel about certain things. It can be painful to wait for someone else to fulfil you or provide you with happiness. You have to learn to be the main provider of your own happiness and use the dating world as a way to have fun and improve certain aspects of your life.

If you look to another person to complete you, you can easily start to lose yourself. How many people do you know that become the person they're dating? Maybe they start liking a certain band or participating in hobbies they wouldn't normally. This is because they use dating as a way to fill part of their life. It's great to be dedicated to someone you love, and to enjoy the same things as them. However, when you let the person you're dating become your identity, you'll eventually have little of yourself left when it's all over.

Your Self-Esteem Has to Improve

One of the most challenging things you might face is learning to love yourself. In our capitalist society, we've been fed lies in order to buy into certain ideas. You're told you're overweight, so then you buy products and services to try and reduce your weight. Women are told their skin is too wrinkled as they age, so millions of dollars are spent a year trying to reduce the appearance of your age. There's nothing wrong with wanting to look your best, but some people take it to the extreme. Since women are told their whole lives how bad they look, of course, those thoughts have seeped into our every day mind. It can be hard to look into a mirror and not be critical of many things you see. It's a challenge, but one you can certainly overcome.

Others can see when you're feeling shy or anxious. You've probably noticed some nervous ticks on others before. Maybe they pick at their fingers or scratch their head. Others can notice this behaviour on you if you show any signs of anxiety. Not only is this distracting, but you also give those around you the notion that what you have to say might not be worth anything. If you don't even believe in yourself, how do you expect others to? We all have moments when we're nervous, but there's nothing more attractive than being secure with yourself. It lets everyone else know that you think you're great, which means you're probably great!

If you don't believe what you have to say, and offer is important, why should anyone else? The type of people who captivate their audiences are those filled with confidence. How many times have you seen an unattractive celebrity and wondered how they got to be so popular? There are plenty of famous people that aren't conventionally attractive, but still wildly successful. This is because they're filled with confidence. They believe in themselves and know that they have something to prove. People respond to this kind of confidence, and anyone is capable of having that power. You just have to navigate your anxieties and insecurities, constantly challenging your thoughts.

Humility cannot be forgotten, so it's about balance. No one likes the guy that thinks he's so great he can do no wrong. You still have to remain humble through your confident streaks, knowing that we're all inherently flawed. People that think their poo doesn't smell, for lack of better terms, seem unrealistic, so there's a lack of relatability. We all love someone that knows their worth, but still knows there's always room for improvement.

It's not easy. You're going to have days when you still hate what you see. You might wake up the next morning after a date and go over and over in your head about everything that you said that was wrong. You'll obsess over pictures that you took or that someone took of you, picking out every little detail that makes you look bad. This is because we've been trained to think this way. It's a habit that was forced into us as we grew up, so unfortunately, those thoughts will always be there. The older you get, the less you'll care, but in the meantime, you can practice building yourself up instead of breaking yourself down.

They'll Be Just as Scared as You

When facing a scary bug, like a spider, your mom might have told you not to be afraid. The spider is just as scared of you as you are of it! This is true about the people you're going to go on dates with. Dating is hard, and that's a pretty common idea. We're not saying anything new by bringing up the insecurities that can flood your brain during a date. Just remember this and know that you're not alone! The person across from you is just as anxious as you are. Maybe a little less, but maybe a little more, too. Don't be afraid to admit that you're nervous either! You don't want to be a blubbery mess, but sometimes just laying it out there can help calm you down. They might share they're nervous too, and the date will likely end up being a lot more relaxing.

Most people are more concerned with what they're doing and saying than what you are. In the moments that you're talking, they're listening, but they're also probably talking to themselves a bit, prepared for what they're going to say next. Maybe that day they spilled something on the shirt they wanted to wear, so now they're uncomfortable in a shirt that's too tight. Perhaps they're not as cute as their picture and they realized you were twice as good looking as they had originally thought. We all have experiences that make us nervous or anxious, so it can be easily assumed that others feel just as scared as you!

They probably won't pick up on the little things. They're just getting to know you. If this is a first date, that means you just met. They don't know your every little move or have predictions about the things you'll do and say. You do! You're with yourself every hour of the day, so you have a better grasp on the things you're doing. You can't expect the person you just met to know as much about you as you do about you. Make sense?

Are you more critical of yourself or others? Some people are way more judgmental of themselves than they are of others. You might think something that you do is stupid, but if someone else does the same thing, maybe you wouldn't think twice about it. Just try and practice treating yourself the way you would a friend. Before you take what you say to heart, would you say the same negative thing to your mom? Your sister?

All those moments of nerves ticking and stomachs turning, they're probably having too. When you're feeling nervous, choked up, or not yourself on a date, just remember that they might be feeling the same way! If they're not, and if they're someone that's way too confident, lacking total humility, you might consider that they wouldn't be someone you wanted to date anyway.

The Importance of Self-Care

An important step on the path to loving yourself is self-care. You've probably heard that word a lot lately. Some people use it as an excuse to take a bubble bath every day, or overeat fast food, but are they that wrong to do so after all? Our time on this planet is so short that we should spend as often as possible feeling good about ourselves! Bubble baths, treating yourself to takeout, and exotic facemasks are a key part in self-care, but know that it also goes deeper than that.

It's not just about doing your hair and wearing makeup. You give so much of your time every day to other people. Wherever you work, there's a good chance that you give someone you barely like 20-40 hours a week of your time. Perhaps you have a family member to take care of and a child yourself. It's important that in all the things you do, you make sure to set aside time for yourself. You don't want to lose who you are. Some think it's selfish to spend so much time alone, but it's important in maintaining who you are. It can be easy for your identity to fade when you give every moment of your life to other people. If you start to love yourself, it'll show! Not everyone has that open of a schedule but be sure to set aside a time at least once a week that you can treat yourself. It doesn't have to be a vacation or day at the spa, but you still need to remember to take care of yourself.

Take yourself on a date! As you navigate through the dating world, you're probably going to spend some money on someone else at a certain point. Why not take yourself on a date instead of someone else? This doesn't mean going to the store to pick up cat litter and getting fast food on the way home. Do something for yourself that you would do for the person you love. Go to a store, and even if you don't have money, take time to look at the things you like. Go see a movie alone and grab a nice dinner after. Pick a movie on TV and do a facemask while you indulge in a big meal. It doesn't have to empty your wallet, but it should be something just a little more special than your every day routine.

It all starts in your mind. Treat yourself the way you would treat the person you love the most. Like we said already, don't say anything to yourself you wouldn't say to a loved one. You're around yourself all day every day. Shouldn't you like that person? Shouldn't you want to treat them to something nice? Why not? This also means taking care of yourself on all levels. Eat healthy not because you want to crash diet, but because you want to feel good inside. Have a special skincare routine not because you want to look younger, but because you want your skin to be soft. Workout not so you can get a body that attracts others, but so it's easier to walk up the stairs and carry groceries from your car to the house. It might seem silly, or even feel selfish at times, but you have to do things for yourself.

Even on your bad days, take an extra step to give yourself some love. The most important thing to do on these bad days is remind yourself that it's OK! If you miss a day at the gym, don't break yourself down and feel guilty over not going. Remember that we all need to take a sick day every once in a while, even if we're not sick. You don't want to get into any bad habits, but that's because you just want what's best for yourself.

If They Leave, Let Them

All of what we discovered in this chapter is important, because if there comes a time that the other person leaves, you have to be strong enough to let them. That can be a big fear in a relationship. Wondering if they're going to leave you can be sickening, especially at the beginning of the relationship. You get used to having them around, wanting them to be there always. It's important to have a high level of confidence so that you know if they do leave, you'll be just fine. It's never easy to watch someone you love walk away, but if they don't love you, you have to let them leave.

If someone doesn't see your worth, that's on them. Once you've spent some time taking care of yourself and realized the amazing person you are, you'll also see that if someone wants to walk away from that, it's their loss. You won't be asking yourself, "what's wrong with me," and instead, "what's wrong with them?" Know that not everyone is meant for each other, and that sometimes, you're going to experience some heartbreak. That doesn't mean you're a bad person, or unlovable. It just means that you haven't hit the moment in the story that you meet your Prince Charming.

If they don't want you, you have to let them go. How many people do you know that tried to desperately get back together with someone that didn't want them in the first place? You will find someone that sees you and knows that they want to be with you. There won't be any guessing games, or moments wondering if they'll change their mind about you. Don't wait around for anyone, because there's always going to be someone waiting for you. It might not happen overnight, but it will happen, so you can't spend anymore time on someone that doesn't want you. The hardest part of letting someone leave that you loved is accepting that you weren't the right one for them. It can be hard to handle but know it doesn't mean anything bad about you. You probably have some friends that you adore, but you wouldn't date them, right? If someone doesn't want to be romantically involved with you, that in no way means you're a bad person.

Sometimes, you're mourning more than just the loss of a person. Maybe you were with someone for years, and then things ended. You probably thought about marriage, kids, and buying a house together. Perhaps you have your entire future mapped out with the person you have to watch walk out the door. Realize that you will find a new future. It can be scary to try and see your future in a different light. If a relationship ends, your next thought will probably be one of fear, wondering if you'll find anyone at all ever again. This is natural, but it doesn't mean that it's true. There will be someone out there, someone that loves you more than the person that decided to leave. Even if you never meet this person, wouldn't it be better to live a life happily alone than trapped in a loveless relationship?

There's always a worry at the end of a relationship that you might have wasted time. It can be hard to give up on something that you've invested time, emotions, and even money into. All the vacations, all the times spent with each other's families can feel like wasted moments if you decide to just end the relationship. You have to get this idea out of your head, however. Every moment you've lived has been important in defining who you are. It's good to have invested time in different relationships, as when you find the one that's right, you'll have all the knowledge from the past to improve your future.

Chapter 3: Finding the Right Partner

Finding someone single who wants to be in a relationship isn't always the hard part. Depending on your location that can certainly be a problem, but realistically, in any 25-mile radius, there's going to be a healthy handful of people that are single. The hard part, however, is that a lot of these people aren't going to be good matches for you. You might end up dating more than you have to in order to realize that, so we want to help make sure you're doing the best to find the partner that will compliment your life perfectly.

Decide What's Right For YOU

What do you want in a relationship? It's easy to look at a partner and know what you want. Someone handsome, with muscles, and the right haircut. That can be great for a fun night, but what do you actually want for your life? Go ahead and make a list of what things you want out of a relationship, not just a partner. Here are some ideas to get you started in case you aren't even sure what you want yourself:

1. A relationship with a lot of laughter.
2. A partnership in which they care for you as much as you care for them.

3. Unbreakable honesty and trust.
4. Constant support and appreciation.
5. The ability to be unapologetically yourself.

These are all things that might not be in every person you find, no matter how ideal they might be. Maybe you want to date a tall dark and handsome doctor with a great house. You could find him tomorrow, but is he going to have all the things on your list of what you actually want from a relationship?

Other people will try to tell you what kind of person to date. Maybe your parents have an idea of the kind of man they want you to end up with. Perhaps you come from a family of politicians, and they want you to marry someone with a notable political science degree. Maybe your mom doesn't want you to date anyone in the music industry, as she had her own heart broken by too many drummers. No matter who other people want you to date, you have to find a person that YOU want to date. It can be hard to tell if you're attracted to someone because they're good for you, or if it's because you *think* they're good for you.

The right person is different for everyone. Maybe you have sisters that all married lawyers. It'd be nice if you did too, but you absolutely loathe lawyers. You can't feel guilty about not being with someone that other people think is right for you.

It's hard to not compare yourself to others, but just remember that Mr. Right can easily be Mr. Wrong for a different person.

Opposites attract, but sometimes dating yourself can work too. You probably know a couple of different romantic partners that seem like complete opposites. Then you might know someone that seems as if they're dating their clone. There's no strict rule to the type of person you should date. You have to define that yourself. If you're strong-willed and stubborn, an opposite might be better. If you're more relaxed and easy-going, a partner that's similar would be ideal. Everyone is different, so you have to accept that everyone's perfect guy is different as well.

At the end of the day, this is going to be a person you're sharing a bed with every night. You might find someone that seems to fill every quality on your mom's checklist. Everyone has a natural desire to please their parents, so maybe you go ahead on a few dates with this person in the hopes that they'll be the perfect one to bring home to your parents. You have to learn to accept that if they're not right for *you*, you have to let them go.

Know What to Look For

When it comes to online dating especially, people will list all sorts of qualities in their biographies. Just because they say they're one kind of person doesn't mean that's true. Everyone thinks that they're the easy-going, fun-loving person of their group. In reality, a lot of people can be pretty unaware of just how uptight or stressed they might be. Take all the qualities you see listed online with a grain of salt. At the same time, it's a good indicator if they have certain qualities listed in their biographies, because at least they desire to be the person they're describing in their biography.

What are the qualities you admire in the friends and family you keep close? This is another good list you could jot down. You have these people close to you for a reason, and if you explore that, it could help when you're looking for a romantic partner. Sometimes, you might not even realize what you're looking for until you look at the people around you. If you're a bold and talkative person, you might assume you want the same. Then you might look at your friends and realize most are a bit more relaxed and quieter. Maybe this is because your bold personality clashes with others. It's important to notice these behaviours so you don't end up picking someone that's completely wrong for you.

Honesty and trust are the greatest qualities. If they're willing to lie about something small, you never know how big of a fib they could be telling. If you end up meeting someone you met online, and they're shorter than they said, consider why they decided to lie. They might have just been insecure with their size and didn't want to get turned down because they're too short. There are other lies that can be concerning, however. If they're going to lie in the beginning, they're going to lie later on as well.

It's important to consider the things you like and dislike when finding a partner. Of course, it seems ideal to find someone that enjoys the same type of music and movies you do. However, you can't depend on this alone to find you the right partner. Having different taste is inevitable. Sometimes, having opposite opinions can add interest in a relationship, especially if you both enjoy critical discussion. Sometimes, others might have not experienced the same things as you, but if you start sharing music and interests, you'll discover you both have similar taste after all. When looking for love online, or even in the real world, it's important to not filter out those that don't love all the same things you do. A true relationship is strong beyond just the things that you both like.

At the end of the day, it's important to trust your gut when looking for the right person. There's a reason you're having that feeling! It's important to experiment with different dates that are opposite of you, but don't force yourself into anything you don't want. If someone is obviously going to be offended or dismissive of the things you like, it's completely fine to not give them a chance. Keep yourself open, however, and always be willing to try new things.

Warning Signs and Other Things to Avoid

How they treat other people is a direct indication of how they're going to treat you. If you go on a date and they're rude to the staff at the bar or restaurant you're in, they likely have little compassion for other people. If they don't seem to have a lot of friends, it might be because no one wants to be their friend. Not everyone has a huge social circle, and that's not a bad thing. You can still tell the difference between someone that doesn't have friends because they're a shy introvert, and someone who's alone because they're a jerk.

Some people think that controlling or jealous men can be a turn on. Unfortunately, there are a lot of women that think it's attractive when their men fight over them. This is just toxic behaviour and a sign that your man sees you not as a person, but as his property. A little jealousy is fine and to be expected. You'd likely be jealous of other women as well, but only to a certain point. If they become aggressive towards another man, or more importantly you, when faced with jealousy, it's best to just run from him ASAP. Being a little protective and jealous is a sign that they at least care about you, but too much proves that they have other tendencies that aren't healthy.

If a guy tells you that you're not like other girls, that's a sign he might be toxic. He's initially grouping all women into one group, seeing them as their stereotypes instead of individual people. If he says you're not like other people, that might be a little nicer rather than grouping you in with all the women in the world. He should see you as an individual person, not as a woman that he's set out to "conquer."

Another good question to ask in the beginning relationship is if they would do the same for you that you do for them. Maybe in the beginning you continue to go to his apartment, bars he likes, or order food that's his favourite. It's nice of you to be caring, but if he's not giving you the same consideration, you need to get out of there quick. If he can't put in the effort in the beginning of a relationship, you can bet it'll only get worse as things progress.

Here are some toxic qualities that could also become potentially dangerous. If you see any of these signs in your date, it's probably best to just avoid these people altogether and end things as soon as possible:
1. They describe one or more of their exes as "crazy"

2. They say something mean but mask it as them "joking"
3. They exhibit any sort of violence on the first or second date
4. They don't tip their bartender
5. They don't want to show any public affection or indication you're dating each other
6. They laugh at any of your dreams or goals
7. You find yourself afraid to share basic information with them
8. They monitor who you hang out with
9. They demand getting texted/called more frequently than you can handle
10. they don't know how to apologize or admit they're wrong

Small Things That Could Lead to Bigger Issues

Some of these might seem like forgivable qualities. Maybe you know someone already that has them, or you've experienced some of the list yourself. We've all made mistakes, but it's important to recognize these early on in a relationship because they could certainly only get worse. When it comes to physical violence or emotional abuse, it's important to leave the relationship as soon as something like this is detected. Abusers can be very manipulative and controlling, so you have to get yourself out before it's too late. Don't ignore the warning signs just because you really feel like you're falling for someone. That's how many people end up trapped in relationships they knew wasn't right in the beginning. It feels so good to start falling in love with someone and it can be easy to forgive the small things you don't like. As time goes on and the relationship progresses, that forgiveness will start to fade, and you'll be left having to confront the problems you spent so much time ignoring.

It can be challenging to look for signs in the blissful stages. When you're falling for someone, you have goggles that only allow you to see this person as a godly figure. They might do something wrong and you think to yourself that it's OK because they do this or that or have other qualities you admire. It can be scary to trust your gut as well but stay true to yourself and do your best to weed out the ugly. If your gut is telling you something isn't right, listen to that, don't pretend you didn't hear.

Think of a new relationship as if you're on vacation. You are having an absolutely amazing time, every step of the way. Maybe you're in a tropical destination or a cool city. You wake up happy, spend every moment having fun, and go to bed excited for more. On every vacation, most of us have an urge to live there! Who hasn't fantasized about just staying on vacation forever? You have to ask yourself, however, if you could actually live where you're vacationing. Could you handle the climate? The lifestyle? It's great at first, but if you actually lived there, it might not be the glamorous trip you imagined. The same can be said for a relationship. The beginning is always great, exploring every part of a new person. However, once that phase passes, is there still going to be something there that you can base a relationship on?

Some love stories seem so unachievable, but mostly because they are! When watching reality TV shows, or romantic movies, you might wonder why you can't have a relationship like that. They seem so in love, and it makes you wonder if what you have with your partner is real. That's because on TV, they don't live real life. They don't go grocery shopping together or share the moments in bed when someone is hogging the covers or snoring too loud. You're not going to find a flawless relationship, so don't compare yours to what you're seeing on TV.

It's OK to fight. Sometimes, it's actually better than not fighting at all. Fighting with someone allows you to think critically with them. It gives you a chance to honestly express your feelings and them the opportunity to do the same. Fighting can ruin a relationship, but it can also make one stronger. Too much fighting or fighting that gets violent is a clear warning sign that the relationship probably isn't right for you.

Don't Be Too Strict with Your Checklist

We strongly encourage you to write a list of the qualities you want in a person. We want you to be writing the entire time that you're reading this, but this is important now, just like the previous list of what you want in a relationship. If you compare the two lists, you might find that you want a completely different person than you originally thought. Some qualities you might consider are the age, appearance, occupation, and location of the person that you want to date. It's good to write these out to help you learn more about yourself and the things you want.

However, you can't use your list of qualities as a strict tool. You're likely not going to find the ideal person you wrote about in your journal. Maybe they have 9/10 qualities, so cutting someone out because they don't meet all ten is a bit foolish. Of course, you shouldn't date someone that's obviously wrong for you, such as an occupation, religion, or general outlook you don't agree with. You should still be open to altering the checklist, understanding that some people might have more qualities you didn't even have listed.

You might find someone that's completely opposite of what you wrote down, so don't let your list block you from exploring that relationship. It can be scary at first, especially if they don't seem to have any of the qualities you originally wanted. There are going to be cases of people like this catching your interest. It's completely OK to explore these relationships.

Have a few core values that you stick to, but don't let it blind you too much when seeking a partner. It's OK to stay strict with some things, especially if you have a religion or occupation that narrows the selection of people. It can be fun to go on dates with people different then you but picture your future and be sure that these differences would still workout in your everyday life.

This isn't just about getting a boyfriend. You want a partner. You don't just want someone that you can have sex with and take good Instagram pictures. You need a guy that will be there for you when you need him, and a guy that loves you as much as you love him.

Chapter 4: Attracting Other People

Your friends and family remind you often, at least they should be, that they'd love and support you no matter what. Unfortunately, the same graces aren't given by potential partners when entering a relationship. People are quick to make judgments. You could have some small behaviour that reminds them of their mother, so forever, they'll classify you as that sort of figure. It's not always going to happen, but you can certainly run into some judgmental men in the dating world. It's certainly the worst part about dating, but it is inevitable.

Putting yourself out there as a single woman means that you're putting yourself in a position to be judged. Many believe that men judge women harder than women judge men, but that line is a lot blurrier than you'd imagine. Most of the time, it's women that judge other women the harshest, but again, that's because what we've been taught in our society. We're all afraid of being judged, because we know deep down that we're so much more than the assumptions people have for us. Sometimes, the fear of judgement holds us back and keeps us from living our dreams! In order to enter the dating world, you have to be attractive to others on some level. With the tools we've already discussed and what we're going to be talking about in the rest of the book, that shouldn't sound so scary to you!

Find Out What Your Best Self Is

Now is the time to write a list of the things that you admire about yourself. This might be one of the most challenging lists to write. If we asked you to jot down everything you want to change about yourself, it might be a lot easier. You could probably write a novel about all the mistakes you've made or embarrassing moments. Who hasn't lied awake at night going over a situation in their head repeatedly? Instead of participating in that toxic behaviour, it's time to look into your mind and pick out the things you like about yourself!

Go ahead and write things you wish to achieve and goals you have for yourself as well. Maybe you want to travel somewhere or write a book! Even if it seems unachievable, write it down. Sometimes speaking things into existence can work! You should have a long list and collection of your positive qualities, your dreams, and your future goals. When we spend so much time tearing ourselves down, it can be hard to find the things that make us who we are. There's a reason why the people in your life that love you do so much! Even if it doesn't seem like it, we all have someone out there that admires us, and there's a reason for that.

Remember to improve yourself because you want to, not because you're trying to keep a man around. That way, if the unfortunate time comes that they do leave, it won't hurt so bad. Finding your best self is a way that you can boost your confidence, another important step in navigating the dating world.

Don't put so much pressure on yourself. Be as forgiving to yourself as you would be to a young child. Don't make yourself feel bad because you might have said the wrong thing. Instead, figure out what you didn't like about what was said and figure out how to improve it for the next time. There's no point in wallowing in self-loathing. It's time to be productive with your thoughts in order to be the best version of yourself possible.

We all have different versions of ourselves, and you have to pick out which one you like the most. Don't be anyone you're not just to fit someone else's idea of who you should be. We have our work persona, the personality we put on for our family, and the wild side that some of our friends can bring out. Work on harmonizing the best parts of these personalities, and you'll discover who you truly are.

Avoid Complaining

When meeting new people, we can often connect easiest by the common hatreds we share. There's a lot of things we could list out that people generally hate. Waiting, war and crimes, paying bills, and annoying political figures. Sometimes, our hatreds can bring us together, so it can be easy to have long conversations with our dates about all the things we both loathe.

It can feel natural and become easy to spend an entire date hating on the same thing. You have to avoid this, however. No one likes spending their time with a complainer. As we've discussed, there are plenty of commonly shared hatreds. Complaining about the weather with a co-worker is a good way to make the day go by a bit faster, but at the end of the shift, do you really feel all that more connected to the person? It's easy to glide through a conversation ripping apart a shared hatred, but it doesn't help you learn anything about the other person.

You can find common traits based in the way you judge and criticize different things, but you don't want to base your relationship on this. You'll get to the negative parts later in the relationship. Right now, take the time to get to know each other. Learn about what makes them happy, not what makes them annoyed. You could also risk having yourself associated with the hatreds discussed on the date. Even though you might've spent that time expressing that you too dislike the same things your date does, it could sour the mood and put a negative twist on the night.

Venting feels great, but it's not the way to start something, especially a relationship you want to build. If you notice that you and your date have been complaining for more than just a couple minutes, try to change the subject and twist it into something positive. Don't be afraid to call out the conversation either, by saying something like, "Instead of us talking about how much we hated the newest Marvel movie, why don't you tell me about a movie you saw recently you liked?" This comment could be used in many different ways and will help let your date know that you're not someone who spends all their time complaining. At the same time, ou don't want that quality in a partner.

Be Nice to The People Around You

Going out to a restaurant for a date seems basic, but there are so many interactions throughout the date that can give you insight to what your partner might be like in the real world. When the hostess tells them that it'll be another 10 minutes before you get a seat, does he roll his eyes, or does he smile and wait patiently? When the server greets you, does he give them a chance to talk or does he cut them off right away and put in his order? It's important that you're making the same effort to be kind to the staff at wherever you decided to have your date. He'll notice your behaviours in this regard the same way that you will.

When you meet someone, it can be hard to not picture what they might be like around their friends and family. They're going to be wondering the same thing, so it can be nice to bring them up as you're talking throughout your date. You can tell them about a tradition you and your friends have, or about the last present you gave your mom for her birthday. These are small and interesting topics that won't take up the entire date, but he'll notice your comments and formulate opinions based on the things you mention. If you bring up a fight you had with your sister on the first date, he might assume right away that you have trouble maintaining relationships with your family members.

How you treat just the bartender alone can give your date huge insight to how you're going to be acting towards them throughout the rest of the relationships, and you should take that into consideration as well. When just ordering a drink, there can be a test of patience, friendliness, and compassion, all within a matter of seconds. Don't let these interactions slide by and take these as opportunities to show him what kind of partner you would be.

If you get to go to their home, or let them into yours, how you interact with pets can be another indicator. I think we can all agree that if his dog likes you, that's a pretty good sign! Go out of your way to show him that you're a kind and considerate person. He'll remember those positive moments and take note of any warning signs he might notice in your interactions.

Just as he'll be paying attention to your interactions, you should be taking mental notes as well!

Ask Questions and Listen to The Answers

A first date is going to be filled with you and the other person asking a ton of questions. You're two people that just met, and who knows if this is the person you're going to be having children with! It's perfectly normal to ask questions, and you should! Trying to get to know the other person means that you care, and they'll realize this. Asking questions is great, because it helps keep the conversation going without the pressure. If there's a moment of silence, don't be afraid to ask them anything, such as what their favourite song or movie might be. They'll be expecting questions like this, so it's not like it'd be a strange thing to do. Don't be afraid to ask unique or strange questions either, as it'll help keep the night interesting! Here are some unique questions you could ask your date when you're feeling uncomfortable:
1. What's the last thing you bought that you regret purchasing?
2. What's an embarrassing story your mom would tell me if I called her right now?

3. If you found out you had to move away tomorrow, where would you go?
4. What's the worst gift you've ever received?
5. What's the best prank you've ever pulled?

Don't turn it into a job interview. You should be having fun and getting to know your date, not grilling them to find out if they meet ever point on your checklist. Make sure that you're actually listening to what they say as well. They'll notice if you're just breezing through and trying to make it to the next question.

You're going to want to ask a lot, and it's completely fine if you write down a list of questions you want to ask before going on the date. Just don't take the list with you, of course. Figure out what else you might want to know about the person before going on the date. Did they share something funny on their dating profile that you need more explanation for? Maybe they shared very little information and you don't know much about them at all.

Listening to the answers is important. Instead of going through the list of things you want to ask, it's important to actually listen to the answers so you can form conversations from that. Maybe you only make it to the first question and the rest of the night is conversation after conversation that flows perfectly. Actually, engaging in a conversation is more important than anything else.

People love talking about themselves! Your date won't be mad if you make an effort to get to know them. Just remember, if they don't share the same curiosities that you do, they might not be right for you. If you notice that you've been doing all the question-asking, it could just be because they're nervous. It could also mean that they're more self-centred than you'd like.

Stay True to You

Remember, you're doing this for yourself! You might have a child already and you're looking for another parental figure for them. Even if that's the case, dating is still about finding the right person for you. You can't compromise who you are or any of the ideas you have just in an attempt to impress someone else. You could go into the date as a completely different person, and maybe they end up liking that fake person. Are you going to keep up the façade for the rest of your life? You have to be yourself, because that's the easiest. If they don't like who you are, they know where the door is.

You're going to have qualities that some people don't like. You could be voted the most beautiful woman in the world, but there's still going to be that one guy that just doesn't find you attractive one bit. Remember, that's his fault, not yours! Never, ever change anything about you to suit someone else. If they don't like who you are, tell them to go find someone they do like. There are even people that don't like pizza or chocolate, so you have to accept that some people just won't like you. Don't let this defeat you. Let it be a reminder that when you do find someone that adores you, it will be amazing.

When it comes to bad habits that you might have, like smoking, your partner might want you to change this. If they express ideas like this, it isn't always bad. You just have to look at what they're asking of you and why they might be doing so. Do they want you to quit smoking because they care about your health, or because they just don't think it's attractive? If someone wants to change your bad habits, that can be an indication that they actually care about you and your health. However, don't let someone convince you that a normal quality you exhibit is a bad habit. If you find yourself compromising who you are or what comes naturally because your date doesn't like that quality, it's a sign they might be too controlling.

It can be hard to be yourself, especially if you're still not even sure who that is. If you stay authentically you, you'll find your way. It's going to be hard, but it's going to be very worth it in the end.

There's no one out there worth compromising who you are for. For every person that you meet that doesn't like you, you'll find two that do! It can be hard to let go of someone that you might be falling for because they don't like you as much. You have to let them go, because if they don't love you for everything you are, they aren't the one.

Chapter 5: Navigating Online Dating

It can be crazy to think of how just a few decades ago, if you wanted to find a date, you might take out a classified ad in the newspaper. They didn't have computers in their pockets and every other technology capable of finding a partner. You might have even had to meet someone, like a dating or relationship expert, before landing a few dates. Nowadays, it seems as though the only way that people meet is online. If you ask couples how they've met, most will say either through work, school, or online. There aren't cute stories of how people met as often, which can be sad sometimes. On the other hand, how lucky are we that we could potentially find a soulmate with the touch of a button? You can select what kind of person you're looking for just as you might a new television you're buying online. That thought can terrify some, but excite others.

If you're not online, you might be a little behind in the dating world. Even if you do meet someone in person, there's a good chance they're already on different dating apps and websites. That's just the way the world works now, and whether you like it or not, it's gotten too big to fight. If you can't beat them, join them. If you're reading this book and you haven't gone online yet, that's your first step. It can be scary, but you'll be shocked to find out just how many people there are in the world that are trying to date you.

You're still going to meet people you might want to date in the real world, but in the society, we live in, it can still be important to get online and go on some dates. You don't have to give up hope that you might find Mr. Right in your favourite coffee shop after a chance encounter. You do have to accept that the world is changing, and the person that's meant for you might be making their Tinder profile right now. There are plenty of people that are resistant to the technological world that surrounds us, but so many have found love through online dating that it's clear we can't fight it any longer.

Tinder Secrets

There is an endless amount of dating sites that you could choose to use. There's even a website specifically for farmers that want to date other farmers. You can make profiles based on your religion, and some sites even help you find a sugar daddy. We have endless options when it comes to making dating profiles, but there are some clear winners that everyone seems to be using. Tinder is certainly a popular choice, and the style of the app is becoming common for other dating sites. Swiping right or left has really simplified the way we look at dating and potential partners. It can seem weird to be able to have this power in your fingertips, so we're going to offer some tips to help you navigate this crazy world.

Never lie on your profile. This is probably one of the most important rules. It can be tempting to crop out your body and use a slimming picture of your face. You might even want to lie about where you work or exaggerate how much time you spent in school. While this is certainly possible to do when making profiles online, you should avoid this at all costs. Lying online only sets you up for future failures. They're going to find out you look nothing like your picture or that you fibbed about how much money you might have. You want someone to fall in love with you, not with a complete stranger. Lying can become tricky in more ways than just getting confronted with the truth. Some people find themselves addicted to the thrill of lying, and end up using somebody else's picture completely, catfishing potential dates. This is not only harmful to the potential date, but you're hurting yourself in the process as well. Nothing good comes from lying, at least long term. It might feel good at first, but you're only going to get yourself in trouble.

Look at it as an outsider. If one of your friends is currently online dating as well, take the opportunity to look at your own page through each other's profiles. Take the chance to see what others see when they click on your profile. Put yourself in the shoes of your potential date, and ask yourself if you didn't know who you were, would you like what you saw? Would you swipe right or left on yourself? You might think you have the best profile you've seen, but when you really take a moment to step back and see your page from an outsider's perspective, you could see exactly what others are seeing.

Ignore people that might try to bug you. You're going to run into people that try to tease you, and maybe take things a little too far online. If it's some harmless joking, do your best to ignore these people. Maybe they'll make a comment about your profile picture, or something silly you had in your biography. If it seems like they're only trying to get a rise out of you, just ignore them. There are plenty of people on the internet that just want attention no matter if it's good or bad, so don't give them any. If someone is legitimately harassing or cyber bullying you, be sure to report them immediately. Even if you don't take personal offense to their harassment, there might be someone else out there that could get serious emotional trauma from an online interaction. Do your best to help weed out the ugly on the different dating apps you're using.

Remember, it's just an app. There are way too many people that can become dangerously addicted to their power to swipe right or left. At the end of it all, remember to not take things too seriously. The outcome of what's happening as you're navigating the online dating world could be very serious, especially if it results in a spouse and children. At the same time, it's an app that you might have stored next to your favourite game. You can't take something like that too seriously. Don't forget that you're supposed to be having fun in this process! If online dating isn't working for you, there are other options, but know that this is certainly the easiest.

Making A Good Profile

Don't go overboard when it comes to creating a dating profile. The more you build yourself up, the higher the expectations your date will have. If you go on and on about how amazingly perfect you are on your profile, your date is going to be expecting that same level of perfection. Don't sell yourself short, but there's certainly a fine line between building yourself up and creating a fake online personality. Don't use only vacation pictures if you don't actually enjoy travelling that often. Nothing bad will happen if you just remain true to who you are and make an honest profile that represents who you really are.

Keep it real. You don't want to seem unapproachable. If you do make a profile that makes you out to be some sort of superhero, you might find that you're not getting as many messages as expected. You could have the best-looking profile compared to everyone else, but fewer messages. You want to make sure that you still seem approachable and as a real person that anyone could date. There will be plenty of guys that would see your meticulously crafted profile and think you might be too good for them. They might fear that you already have too many male suitors and not even make any effort at all. Make sure that your online profile reflects a real person that isn't too scary to reach out to.

Avoid using selfies. Selfies are great. Who doesn't like taking pictures of themselves? When it comes to online dating, profiles that don't have selfies as their main picture end up doing better. Anyone could take a picture of themselves, but not everyone could go for a hike, or party at a cool brewery. Try to use pictures of you doing things as your main profile. If you just use another picture of your face, you'll be grouped in with the rest of the girls that just have pictures of their faces. Instead, use a photo of you in a cool setting, or holding a cute pet. Show people that you do something other than take pictures of yourself.

Always have an original biography. You might find a joke online that you think is funny, but so have ten other people in your area. Nothing is a bigger turnoff than being confronted with a person just like everyone else. If you use someone else's quote, joke, or rip off a biography entirely, you're letting potential suitors know that you don't have much originality. Make sure that you craft a completely authentic biography so as to really stand out. If you can't think of a funny joke, that's totally fine. The cheekiest biographies aren't always the ones that get the most messages. You can prove you're funny later.

Swipe right as often as possible. If you're not sure about a person, swipe right. If they seem perfect but look kind of funny in their picture, swipe to keep them. The worst that could happen is that you don't match. That doesn't mean you shouldn't try in the first place. Obviously, if they're doing something offensive in their picture or their biography, avoid them at all costs. Don't swipe someone away forever just because there was something small you didn't like about them. You might see something that turns you off, but there's always a chance that you're just misinterpreting something small. Give everyone a chance until they give you a bigger reason not to. Who knows if you've already swiped away your soulmate because you saw a poster on the wall in the background of their profile picture. Maybe they were just taking a picture at someone else's house! It's always worth it to just give everyone a shot, even those you would least expect to be attracted to.

Meeting Online People IRL

Never meet anyone at their home. This goes without saying, but for real, make sure that your first meeting with an online date is in public. No one that ends up in a sketchy situation ever thinks that they're going to be the one to wind up there. It might seem lame to be cautious, but it's even lamer to wind up dead or hurt when you didn't have to. As a woman, you have to be especially careful before meeting up with someone. Make sure you discuss the bar or restaurant you're going to and do your research before you go. Be sure it's in an area that has plenty of other activity happening around as well to avoid going to the middle of nowhere. Figure out a plan should you have to leave early. Is there public transportation or a safe spot to park your car? Could you take a cab or Uber should you have to? You might end up really liking the person and wanting to go home with them right away but be sure to be extremely safe about every decision you make when meeting an online friend in person.

Tell at least two people where you're going to be. You might not want to share that you're dating with certain people. Friends might get too nosy, and your parents might get too excited. You don't always have to tell people you're going on a date. Just mention you're meeting a friend for the first time and you want to make sure you have backup should you need it. We're not telling you this to scare you. There's a good chance you could go on fifty dates and never once run into danger. There's also a chance that the first and only date you go on could be one that turns bad quick. You never think it's going to happen to you. You never assume that you're going to be put into a potentially dangerous situation, but it can happen. You shouldn't fear or expect it, but just be prepared should it happen.

Don't have expectations too high. Picture this: you meet the perfect guy online, or so you think. You spend a week or so chatting with them online, eventually getting their number. He asks you on a date and you agree, blissfully telling your friends and family that he's the one. Everything you saw online about him was perfect, and his profile pictures are to die for. Once you finally meet him, however, you realize he has a strange voice and his teeth are a little more crooked than in the pictures. It's going to happen. You're going to meet people that are different than your perceptions, and you have to be ready for that. Our brains do a good job of filling in the blanks between the pictures and information we've gathered about a person online. They don't always create the right picture, however. Don't have expectations for a person set so high that when you meet them, you get disappointed. There are going to be things about them that you guessed exactly right, but there are also going to be some differences you weren't expecting.

Be honest at the end of the night. If you had a terrible date and hope to never see that person again, you don't have to say those exact words, but let them know that'll be the last date. You can think of something to soften the blow, or just tell them straight up you don't think you're right for each other. Save the other person the agony of wondering how things went at the end of the date. Maybe they'll even be able to convince you to go on a second date, even though you were already planning on ghosting them halfway through the dinner. Also, be sure to be honest if you know that you really liked the person. Tell them honestly that you hope to see them again. You can gauge their reaction to see if they feel the same way instead of staying up all night for the next three days, wondering desperately when they're going to text you. Honesty up front only means that you're setting a precedent for honesty later.

Don't delete your profile right away. So, you finally go on a date that really makes you feel something. There's an undeniable gut feeling that HE IS THE ONE. Before you go picking out wedding dresses and deleting all your online dating profiles, give yourself a little reality check. You're going to have a lot of good first dates. You'll have a lot fewer good second dates, and even fewer good third dates. It's going to seem great at first, but don't let yourself get too caught up in a fantasy. It can be easy to build something up only to watch it desperately crumble right after.

There's No Rush

If you meet someone you really like, you might start to feel the pressure to talk to them immediately, set up another date ASAP, and, like we've previously discussed, delete your online dating profiles. You can't rush into things, however, as you still need to be careful. You might feel the pressure that they could be going on other dates when you're not together. You might worry yourself by thinking that he's going to swipe right on another girl right after he does you. If it's the real deal, it's going to find a way. Don't put pressure on the relationship right away, or else you're going to set yourself up for heartbreak.

The person that you might be falling for isn't going to leave you overnight. If he does, well good riddance. If he didn't feel as strongly for you as you did for him on the first date, then it's probably for the better that he decided to move onto someone else. Don't put so much pressure on the relationship right in the beginning. You can't expect him to have the same feelings right away. Some people take more time than others to realize what they want and what they have.

If you put too much pressure on something, it's going to break. Don't force yourself into something you're not sure about just because you're feeling the pressure.

Go at your own pace. Never let anyone force you into an uncomfortable situation. Just as we're warning you to take things slow, make sure your dates offer that same luxury for you. Don't let someone make you feel as though you owe them anything. If someone's pressuring you into a relationship you're not ready for, don't submit just out of fear or guilt. You have to trust your gut, and the right person would never make you do anything you didn't want to. You want to date someone with patience and understanding, so if they're forcing you to agree to a relationship you're not ready for, they're clearly lacking both of those qualities.

Be Safe with An Open Mind

Your safety is the most important thing at the end of the day. Interacting with other humans can always be potentially dangerous, but you can't live your life in fear. You do, however, have to live your life as prepared as possible. You never want to get blindsided by a potentially harmful situation. People can be very manipulative and controlling. You might not realize you were tricked until it's too late. Not only can people be potentially violent, they can also be con artists that use you for money. Never give anyone money online, but that should also go without saying.

There are plenty of people that form relationships with others online just so they can get some bills paid or extra spending money. If someone asks you for money before you meet, there's a good chance that's all they're after. You have to protect yourself in more ways than one.

Online dating is pretty strange. You can find yourself in an odd situation that might seem unexplainable. You put pictures of yourself online, let others decide if they want to date you, and then you meet them, sometimes in a place you've never been before. We do some strange things for love, but it's clear that it's worth it in the end. If love was meaningless and finding a partner wasn't important, people wouldn't be spending all this time and money on dating.

You still have to have an open mind. You're going to have some random encounters and it's not always going to be easy. The prize at the end is so amazing, however, that putting up with everyone can be worth it all.

Don't be afraid to send the first message! Sometimes, for women especially, it can be scary to send the first message. You might be afraid that it seems too desperate or needy to be the one reaching out. There are plenty of guys that like when a girl makes the first move! Who knows if a guy is too shy to reach out as well. You never want to miss out on something potentially amazing just because you're afraid of what could happen. The worst thing you could experience is not getting a message back!

Chapter 6: Some Dating Tips You'll Actually Use

You can google dating tips, ask your friends for advice, or buy countless books on dating. There might be some helpful information, but a lot of tips are unrealistic, or give you advice in areas that aren't really needed. We have some legitimate tips for you that will actually work.

Keep in mind, that everyone is different. There aren't any exact rules of how to do things, so don't put too much pressure on yourself. We've said that a lot in this book, but it's incredibly true. You can't be too hard on yourself during a process that's already challenging enough. Even though everyone is different, these are some dating tips that will help everyone.

Getting Ready Before

Don't decide what to wear until the day of. You might have the urge to go out and buy a new outfit for your date but try to resist. Some new shoes or a cute dress might help, but don't rely fully on a brand-new outfit for your date night. Instead, wait until you wake up the day of the date to see how you're feeling. Each day is different, and you never want to assume what your mood might be. You might wake up wanting to wear something plain and simple, or perhaps it's a day to be adventurous. Wait until you see how you're feeling on the day of the date to make sure that you're as comfortable in what you're wearing as possible.

Now's not the time to experiment with your hair and makeup. Maybe you've always wanted to wear red lipstick but were never brave enough. There's a time and place to experiment with your hair and makeup, and the day of your first date is not that time, unfortunately. You don't want to make yourself anymore nervous or anxious than you already might be. If you try something new, you might end up focusing on that the entire date rather than any conversations you're having. You might try a new hairstyle, only to realize that the restaurant is humid, and it made your 'do completely fall apart. Just keep it simple and work with what you're used to. Experiment new looks with your friends and other people that are willing to be a little more honest!

It's perfectly fine if you want to have a drink or two. While you're getting ready is a great time to pour a glass of wine or mix a cocktail. Put on some music that makes you feel good about yourself and have fun getting ready. A drink could certainly relax you but remember to keep it limited. You don't want to show up already drunk! The same goes for when you're actually on the date. You'll probably be nervous to the point that you're going to want to do a round of shots.

Make sure to not drink too much, as you might end up embarrassing yourself or doing something you regret. Being nervous is uncomfortable, but it's better than getting so drunk you don't even remember the date.

Make sure to spend some time alone during the day before the date. You don't want to forget yourself in this process. Have a moment alone, even if it's just twenty minutes, to just relax and zone out. Maybe take some time to look over all the lists we've had you write so far while reading this book. Be sure to check in with yourself and make sure that you're staying true to who you are.

Always Show Up

There are going to be some days that you just want to no call and no show your date. You might have had a bad day at work and all you want to do is go to bed when you get home. You might find yourself regretting scheduling the date. Maybe it's the only thing you have to do that day and the thought of going makes you so nervous that you want to cancel the occasion. Don't let yourself treat the date like a responsibility. No matter what you might be feeling before the date, just go! Force yourself to get out of bed or off the couch. You don't want to miss out on meeting Mr. Right because you were too lazy to take a shower!

Get ready for the date and actually show up to the bar. Maybe you're regretting the date because it's with someone that you just don't see yourself with. At least get ready for the date and start to head there before cancelling. This way you can see if the nerves about the date are because of who you're meeting or just because you didn't want to have to leave your home.

If you still feel like it's just not the right person for you, go ahead and cancel. There's no use in wasting each other's times. At this point, you should still be ready to go, so maybe you could head to a different bar and have a drink alone. This could be your chance to at least take yourself on a date. Never let yourself cancel on account of not wanting to go out. You're going to have lazy nights where you just want to stay in your pyjamas, but that's not how you're going to meet Mr. Right! Save those pyjama nights for when you're months into the relationship and you have someone next to you to binge your favourite TV shows. Now is the time to do things that scare you!

Be sure that you're cancelling because it's not right, not because you're just scared. Even if you have to cancel last minute, at least you can't say you didn't still try. If you're unsure about the person, still go on the date to make sure that you're giving them a chance. You might find that it's the best date of your life. You would never want to wonder if you cancelled on the person that you're supposed to end up with.

Make sure to tell them you're not going to make it and be honest. It can be awkward to have to cancel, but it's better than completely ghosting them. Getting stood up on a date can be pretty painful. If you leave someone to sit alone at a bar and wonder where you are, it could really kill their spirit. You don't want to make someone else feel as though there's something wrong with them.

Who Pays?

For decades, it's been assumed that the man is going to pay. This mostly stems from men being the providers and women being the ones to work from home. While that's still true for some people, the majority of women in the dating world have their own jobs now and can provide for themselves. We have to wonder now if this means that the days of expecting for the man to pay are over? Women still only make change on the dollar when it comes to the overall statistics of American gender economics. However, since it's 2018, it's time to question what it might mean if the woman decides to pay instead of the man.

It's up to you how to go about the date, and there are different meanings behind what you might choose. It's completely up to you and your date when it comes to deciding who is going to pay. There's no wrong way to do things, and whatever you're most comfortable with is completely fine. A good rule of thumb, in case you're not sure, is to let whoever did the inviting pay. So, if he asks you to go out for drinks, let him pay! If you decide to make the first move and schedule a date, you should be ready to pay for the both of you. He might still want to pay if you take him out, and vice versa. Let's talk about what that could mean to your date.

Letting him pay is completely fine. It doesn't mean you're a submissive woman, or not a true feminist. Some women fear that if they let a man pay, he'll be expecting something at the end of the night. This is complete bogus. You don't have to have sex with someone just because they paid for your drinks and meal. If he is someone that actually expects this, then don't give him any and let him leave. At least you'll get some free drinks in the process! If you want him to pay no matter what, a good trick is to go to the bathroom once you're expecting the bill to come. This way, he'll be left alone with the bill and he has to make the decision on his own.

Splitting the bill is another great way to set a precedent for the future. He might be the type of guy that needs to pay to feel better about himself, so you can let him if he must, but offering to split the bill at least lets him know where you both might stand in the relationship. It's a good way to show that you're in it just as much as he is. Don't force yourself into this situation if you can't afford it, however. If you went somewhere really nice and it's clear he has more money than you, offer to pay for the tip. It shows that you're concerned about what the waitstaff is getting, and that you're willing to help out a bit, but only as much as you can. If he's a lawyer and you're on a cashier's salary, it doesn't make sense to split the $200 bill. Paying the $40 tip could really show him that you're not there just for financial support.

If you decide to pay, that tells him right away what kind of woman he's going to be dating. You let him know from the first date that you're an independent woman and you won't be needing any of his financial assistance. For some men, this is a complete turn-on. How many dates do you think he's been on where the girl forced him to pay by slipping away to the bathroom once the bill came? Now he gets the chance to enjoy the night without having to pull out his credit card. Who knows, maybe you'll make him wonder if he has to give something up at the end of the night. Only joking of course. Be careful if you do decide to pay, as some men might think this is a turn-off. There are certain men that feel the need to provide. They might want to pay to fill some part of their ego. If you want to avoid this kind of man, paying is a good idea in order to scare them away.

Don't Do Anything You Don't Want

Let's not beat around the bush, sex is a big part of what both people are seeking when they go on a date. If you're seeking out someone to become your life partner, you have more on your mind when meeting them than if they're good in bed. You can't deny that the thought pops into your head a few times throughout the date. You two won't talk about it until it comes to the end of the night, but the thoughts will still be there. Just make sure that you don't go into the date with any expectations or pressures. You might want to prepare yourself in case it does happen by doing some extra grooming or stashing some overnight clothes in your bag, but never assume that you're going to be having sex on the first date. You can't make a decision for yourself, for your body, before you meet the person.

There's no written rule anywhere that says you have to sleep with someone on the first date. There's also no rule that says you can't go ahead and jump into bed with them right away. We hear all sorts of pressures and rumours about what the unspoken rules of dating are. Just know that there is absolutely no rule, law, or any sort of demand anywhere that says you have to do a certain thing on the first date. It is your body, so you decide what happens with it at the end of the night. Remember that this is true from the moment you go on the date to wherever you end up that night. If you agree to go back to his apartment after the date for more drinks this DOES NOT mean that you have consented to anything sexual. Don't ever let him make you feel this way. Even if he bluntly asks if you want to have sex and you say yes, you can change your mind at any time.

The most important decision you can make on that night is one that makes you the most comfortable. It doesn't matter if it's the sixth date and you two are already laying naked in bed with each other. If you don't want to have sex, DON'T. Someone that actually cares about you would never force you into an uncomfortable situation. Also, don't let him try and convince you that "blue balls" is a real thing. Even if it were, offer up a bag of ice, not your body for him to use. He'll survive, and if he doesn't, then that's on him. It's not your fault because you didn't want to have sex with him.

If he gets upset that you don't want to have sex, let him be mad. If he threatens to leave, or to go find someone else that will have sex with him, LET HIM LEAVE. Even if it's someone you've already invested a lot of time and money into, you can't be forced to do something you don't want to. You don't want to have to give any of yourself or your time to a man that just wants to use you. Make sure that he knows that no means no. Don't let him berate you and ask you over and over again to have sex until you're so beaten down that you just say yes to get it over with. This is not OK. It might seem obvious when reading this, but many women don't realize they're in a dangerous situation until after the fact. It can be hard to recognize what's going on at the time, but if you feel uncomfortable at all, just leave. If he's worth keeping around, he'll understand.

If he thinks you're any kind of woman because you had sex, let him leave now too. You might have the anxiety that if you sleep with him on the first date, he'll form his own opinion on you. If you want to have sex with him and he wants it too, go for it! You're both consenting adults and you should be having fun. If you're worried that he's going to judge you, think you're easy, or not want to have a committed relationship with you, don't stress. If that is who he really is, then you don't want him anyway. You don't want to date someone that thinks a woman is any less just because she's had more sexual partners. A man that really loves and cares about you would do so whether you've slept with 1 man or 100 men.

It's Supposed to Be Fun

The only way to online date wrong is when you're not having fun! We've discussed a ton of different tips, tricks, and secrets up until this point. Remember that none of them are rules, regulations, or some sort of unwritten law. These are all just suggestions and tips to help make sure you're having as much success and fun as possible. You don't have to listen to what we're saying, just listen to your gut! It's all about you at the end of the day and finding something that improves your life. It's going to be stressful at times, and you might even end up hurting at one point. The overall idea is still to just have fun, so if you're not doing that, you might want to reevaluate why you're doing this in the first place.

Take a break if you have to, there's no pressure. If you've gone on ten dates and you just don't have it in you to go on anymore, it's completely fine to take a break. It's not a race, so don't force yourself to keep going if you don't want to. Someone once said, "love is like a fart. If you have to force it, it's probably shit." It's a pretty lame saying, but it's true! Love isn't going to be easy all the time, but it shouldn't be that hard. Sometimes, when we're desperately looking for a partner is when we have the worst luck. When you're least expecting it, you might end up finding the love of your life.

Be honest with yourself before everything else. You might find someone that you really like, but on the fourth date, you're not feeling that romance anymore. Just because you've invested time into someone doesn't mean you have to stay. Getting hurt is no fun, but sometimes, having to hurt someone else is the hardest part. You have to be honest with yourself, and don't force yourself into a relationship you don't want just because you feel guilty. You don't owe anyone anything. Well, you do actually owe yourself something, and that's happiness. You deserve happiness and you deserve to be loved. Any situation that makes you feel like this is unachievable is not the right one for you.

Find someone that makes you laugh. In all the couples that you know that have seemingly lasted a lifetime, what's one thing they have in common? There's a good chance that they make each other laugh, a lot. You should find someone that does the same thing for you. You don't have to go out and find your local stand-up comedian but look for someone that you can joke with. Find a person that understands your sense of humour, not one that makes you feel bad about the dirty jokes you might make. You could find someone that has a mansion, and endless amount of money, the body of a pro-athlete, and the face of a Greek god, but if they don't make you laugh, are you really going to find happiness with them?

You're allowed to just be friends. Sometimes it can be hard to end a relationship because you genuinely enjoy hanging out with that other person. Just know that becoming friends is an option! Be honest with them and say that the romance isn't there but that you just want to spend time with them. It might be weird at first, but only if you let it become awkward! Don't stay in a romantic relationship you don't want just because you don't want to let that person go. If there's a connection there, you two will find a way to be friends.

Chapter 7: Maintaining the Relationship You Worked For

You did it! You found someone you actually want to be around, and they like you back! It was probably a lot of work, some compromise, and an endless number of butterflies in your stomach. Just know that not everyone will find this in their lifetime. Some people will go forever without meeting someone they like. Others might end up stuck in a relationship that never completely fulfils them. You made it to this point, and we're going to let you know how to best keep up your newfound romance.

Dating was hard but maintaining this relationship can be just as challenging. There are going to be moments of questioning and days you just want to give up. Remember that living with yourself can be hard enough. You have moments where you're too hard on yourself, or days that you can't even get out of bed. You have to realize that those same feelings and doubts are going to pop in with the person that you're becoming closest with. There are going to be moments of doubt when you wonder if there's someone better out there. This is completely natural but it's no reason to end your relationship.

If you're in love, it shouldn't be that hard, but understand that no relationship is easy. There might be a time when you realize that the good parts no longer outweigh the bad anymore. It might be time to let go, but don't give in so easily. We're going to help you navigate through this relationship with the following tips.

Know Your Voice and Use It

The worst kind of partner you could find is someone that doesn't listen to you. Sometimes your emotions might be a little crazy and you might have days when you're acting a bit irrational. Your partner should still listen to your feelings and validate them as often as possible. You're never wrong for having the feelings that you do. What matters is how you handle those feelings. Your partner should be someone that you're willing to talk to and someone that you're not afraid to share your thoughts and fears with. Even if you're having doubts about the relationship, you should be able to go to your partner with these fears without being scared of how they'll react.

You might become more submissive as the relationship goes on. You've invested so much time, and now you don't want to lose them by doing or saying the wrong thing. Something that might have bugged you in the beginning you stay quiet about now just to keep the peace. It happens and it's completely normal to want to just stay quiet about something that makes you upset to avoid a fight. Know that when this does happen, you should still voice your opinion. You don't want to be forced into a corner in your relationship with no way to talk yourself out. Don't let your partner make you feel as though you have to put up with what they do just because you're afraid of losing them. That's not what a relationship should be.

A relationship is filled with compromise. Know that you're going to have moments that you have to sacrifice certain things for your partner. One of the worst parts of being in a relationship is having to share! You might want to eat the dessert all by yourself, but your boyfriend or husband might ask for a bite. Just wait until you have kids! In a good relationship, however, compromise should be easy. You should want to share with this person not because you have to, but because you want to. The sacrifices you make shouldn't cause you too much pain and turmoil because you know that you're doing so to make someone you love happy. If it gets to a point that you feel as though you're sacrificing too much, you might want to take a step back and look at the bigger picture. Is your partner being too selfish? Are they not compromising just as much as you? Your relationship should be 50/50 and if it's not, it's time to question what it's all worth.

Don't let anyone make you feel as though what you're stating is wrong. We've set it before and we'll say it again: you're not wrong for feeling the way you do. How you handle those feelings is what's important. Let's look at this through an example. Your boyfriend tells you that he's going to a party and you know that one of his ex-girlfriends is going to be there. You can't go because you're working. The feeling you might have first is jealousy. THIS IS OK. You're allowed to be jealous, especially if he's going to be around someone he was once in a relationship with. What might not be OK, is how you choose to handle that feeling. If you decide to call in sick to work so you can secretly follow him to the party and watch every move he makes from a bush outside a window, well, that's kind of crazy. How you should handle it is by being honest with your partner and let him know you're feeling a little jealous. If he makes you feel bad about being jealous, that's wrong. Instead, he should offer reassurance that you have nothing to worry about. What you feel is never wrong, it's just how you handle those feelings that could cause issues.

How he handles your feelings is important as swell. Gaslighting is a huge problem in relationships. Gaslighting is when someone makes you feel as though you're crazy for having the feelings that you do. Your partner might be gaslighting you if they manipulate your own feelings to trick you into thinking that your sanity is unstable. If he uses any of these phrases when confronting him about your feelings, he might be gaslighting you.

1. You're too sensitive
2. You're being crazy
3. I'm sorry that you feel that way
4. You're remembering things wrong
5. You always do this
6. Here we go…
7. You're making things up
8. You're getting too upset over this
9. What about what you did to me?
10. Can't you just let things go?

You're Going to Have to Compromise

Compromise is more than just watching a movie or eating at a restaurant that you don't really want to. It might be going to their hometown for Christmas since they haven't seen their mom in five years. Maybe it's not drinking around them because they're a recovering alcoholic. In order to enter in a relationship, you have to expect to be selfless at times, because they should be giving the same treatment back to you.

You have to make sure that they're giving just as much as you. When making a big decision that could seriously affect your life, always ask if they would do the same for you. Maybe they got a job in California and want you to move with them, but you have no friends or family on the west coast. This would be a huge lifestyle change, but for the right person, it could happen. Before you pack your bags, ask yourself if they would do the same thing for you? If the answer is no, you're likely compromising too much for your relationship.

Don't avoid fighting too much. Sometimes it can be easier to just stay quiet and give in to what your partner wants to avoid fighting. DON'T DO THIS. Every once in a while, you might just to make the night go by easier, but don't let this become a habit. If you do, and then you finally decide to stand up for yourself, your partner will be confused. They'll see you as combative or ask why you didn't bring things up sooner. Not wanting to fight is normal, but sometimes, it's going to happen. Fighting can actually improve your relationship way more than just keeping quiet.

Sex isn't something you should have to compromise. If you have a high libido and your partner doesn't, you might have to compromise by having less sex. Don't put pressure on someone to do something they don't want to do. If it's the opposite, however, never compromise your body just for someone else's pleasure. At one point in time, especially in the online dating world, you might meet a guy that claims he has to have sex every night in order to fall asleep. Don't buy into this. If you want to have sex every night, more power to you! Don't let your partner guilt you into having sex if you don't want to. This should never be a compromise.

Know the difference of compromising with someone and being controlled by them. Again, if you feel like you might be compromising too much, go back to the gaslighting list we had previously discussed. Is your partner saying things like that to you when you ask to get what you want? If so, it might be time for some revaluation.

Keep It 50/50

You have to remember that your lover is supposed to be a partner. They're not there to just take care of you, and you're not there to just take care of them.

50/50 means more than just splitting things in half. Picture your relationship as a cake. Let's say you've spent the day eating cake and ice cream, and your partner hasn't had cake in months. When it comes time to split the cake up, you might want to give them more slices than you'd take yourself. Does that make sense? It's not always about just cutting things down the middle. That doesn't always mean sharing. You're going to want to look at the situation as a whole and figure out how to maintain equality.

Sometimes, there might not be a balance. Maybe they're going through something hard. If they lost a family member or got laid off from their job, they're going to need you. For a while, maybe even months at a time, you're going to give 90 when they can only give 10. This is expected. The key is to make sure that things eventually go back to 50/50, and when it comes time for you to only give 10 percent, they're willing to give 90.

You shouldn't mind giving them a little bit more. This is the person that you love more than anyone. This is your life partner. Of course, you're going to want to give them more than just a little bit. If you feel as though it's been unbalanced consistently, it might be time to do some revaluation.

Be Supportive

You have to remember that the relationship isn't just about finding someone that supports you. You have to offer that same love back. Even if you might not fully believe in something they do, you should still offer the love and support needed for them to follow through with their passions.

You always have something to offer. Just because you're broke and your partner needs money to fix their problems doesn't mean you don't have anything to offer. Just letting someone know that you're there and rooting for them can be all the support they need.

It can be hard to be supportive. Sometimes you don't have the effort to support yourself, so how can you be expected to help someone else? If you feel as though you can't offer the support they deserve, let your partner know this. Say something like, "I'm sorry, I know you have a show coming up, but I just don't think I have the mental strength to go. I love you and believe in you, but I'm not emotionally available right now." Someone that loves and cares for you will understand that this is OK. It should become a consistent bad habit, but you're not going to be able to always give %100, all day every day.

Don't let them give up on their dreams. Even if they seem crazy, you should support them endlessly. If they want to become an astronaut even though they're 40 years old with no college education, tell them they can do it! They might not ever follow through, but it's still important that your partner knows that you love them endlessly.

Don't talk badly about them when they're not around. You can easily grow resentment if you spend too much time gossiping about your partner. You're going to want to gossip and vent a little bit to your girlfriends or maybe your mom. It's OK to share the small things that annoy you or even some larger fears you have. Make sure to still monitor just how much you're sharing about the other person. You don't want to grow hatred for them and make everyone around you hate them too. They're not there to defend themselves, and if you only ever share negative things about your partner with your friends, they're not going to like them either.

Don't Be Afraid to Show Affection

Don't let anyone make you feel bad about showing your partner affection and love. People sometimes get teased for showing too much PDA, but really, anyone who judges you that much has probably never had a positive relationship. We're not saying to go and make out with your partner in the middle of the grocery store. But never be afraid to give a small peck, or even hold your partner's hand. It's not silly or stupid to show someone how much you love them. It can feel good to your partner to know that you want to show them off.

Sometimes, this is the best support you can offer. If you don't have money, time, or something else they need, you always have a sweet kiss or a hug to offer them. Just these small reminders that someone else loves them can really help them through some of their darkest moments.

Human touch can cure all. If you're feeling distant from your partner, don't be afraid to tell them. Hold their hands while you have serious conversations, so they know that you still love them. Hold them while they sleep to help ease their nightmares while they're slumbering. Even a simple touch on the shoulder can really turn someone's mood around.

You don't have to be sexual to be intimate. Don't feel like kissing, making out, or cuddling has to lead to sex. These moments can actually be a little more intimate than if you did have sex. Holding each other and just feeling another person's warmth can really bring you closer.

Be respectful of others, but don't compromise when it comes to spoiling your partner. You don't want to be so obsessed with PDA that you become the couple that makes everyone uncomfortable. Just remember to never let anyone make you feel guilty about showing your partner some love.

Here are some small gestures that can really show your partner you love them.
1. Buy their favourite candy bar next time you're at the grocery store checkout
2. Highlight a part in a book you're reading that you want them to read
3. Do the dishes for them if you notice their sink is overflowing
4. Pick some wildflowers as you walk to your house. Even guys appreciate flowers every now and then!
5. Drop their favourite coffee drink off at work for them.

6. Leave post-its in their car or on their bathroom mirror that remind them how much you love them.
7. Always kiss them as you're saying hello, goodbye, goodnight, and good morning.

Chapter 8: Applying All This to Real Life

You're almost done! Once you've finished the book, it's time to start dating in the real world. We've given you a ton of information, and hopefully you've been paying attention! Taking notes is always key, and if you haven't been doing so, you haven't missed your chance yet. It can feel silly to take notes and study a book about dating. Some people feel like it's desperate or pathetic to be doing research about dating. Don't ever let anyone make you feel this way, especially yourself! It just shows that you care and that you actually want to get to know someone on a deeper level.

Reading a book is easy but putting yourself out there isn't going to be. Anyone can skim through a book and take away the important parts. Now you're going to be put to the test and you're going to have to apply all of the ideas we've discussed to your real life. It can be scary, but we're not abandoning you just yet! Here are some tips to make your transition from reader to doer!

Start Fresh with New Profiles

There is a reason that things haven't been working out so far. Maybe you've already been dating online for months now and you have yet to even go on a date. Part of it might be your own subconscious fear, but part of it might also be that you don't have a very attractive profile. Go ahead and delete all your profiles right now and start completely fresh. Rewrite your biography, take some new pictures, and just start completely over.

Instead of going back to your profiles and changing them to fit what we've talked about, don't be afraid to start fresh. It can be scary to delete different ideas, especially if you've been altering your profiles for months. Sometimes, just breathing new energy into something can be enough to make it that much more attractive. This is your time to become a new version of yourself. Leave behind the past and prepare for a brighter and better future!

Take some new pictures! You're a new person after reading this all, aren't you? We mentioned already to try and avoid selfies, but if that's all you got, that's fine too. If you're not one to take selfies, don't be afraid to let someone else take a picture of you. Next time you're at a park, walking down a cool part of the street, or getting a cup of coffee at your favourite spot, don't be afraid to ask a stranger to snap a quick picture. You'll likely never see them again, so don't be afraid to put yourself out there. Who knows, you might end up hitting it off with the person that takes your picture too! You can then use these candid's as engaging and unique profile pictures for different dating apps.

Don't google what to put in a biography. Just be true to yourself. Originality is one of the most attractive qualities. Don't put too much pressure on having something funny or witty in your biography if that's not the kind of person you are.

Be unapologetically yourself! This is the most attractive thing to other people. If you believe in yourself, so will everyone else!

Write A Letter to Yourself

We told you to write a letter to your exes to help get over them. Now it's time to write a letter to yourself. It can seem weird but grab a pen and paper and sit down to take a moment to write something to yourself, for yourself. Don't just pull out your notes app on your phone and make a list. Sit down and write a letter!

Remind yourself of how strong you are. There are going to be moments that you just want to give up but having a physical reminder you can look at will help get you through those dark periods. Remind yourself of all the great qualities you have and the people in your life that love you. No one is going to be reading this but you, so don't be afraid to go overboard. Give yourself the love you deserve! Remind yourself you're a Rockstar, a badass, a superwoman, because guess what: YOU ARE.

Writing things down can help you articulate what you're feeling. We have so many thoughts swirling through our brains at all times, that taking a moment to really write everything out can change a lot! You can keep this list around to remind you of how great you are when you're feeling down.

Oppositely, you can also write a letter to yourself about everything you hate. Write a letter saying how much you hate the way you look, or how often you feel like you embarrass yourself. It might hurt, and you might make yourself cry. Even though it's hard, do it. Once you're done with the letter, you might realize just how awful you can be to yourself. Would you give that same hateful letter to the 5-year-old version of yourself? Once you're done with the letter, rip it up, burn it, pulverise it into a bloody pulp. Whatever you do, get rid of that letter because you're done talking to yourself like that.

Make Some Lists

We've gone over a lot in this book and we've told you to do quite a few different things. You might feel overwhelmed, but that's good! This isn't going to be easy. Nothing that's worth it in the end is ever easy.

To remind you of what we've discussed in the book, here's a list of some lists that you should try writing:

1. Qualities you want in a partner.
2. Things you want out of a relationship
3. Things you admire about your family and friends
4. Things you admire about yourself
5. A list of your dreams and goals for the future (no matter how big or small)
6. Questions to ask on a first date

Chapter 9: Having Fun with It All

You're here because there's something missing in your life, right? When you see other people walking down the street and holding hands, maybe it hurts a little. Perhaps you're tired of showing up to parties and weddings alone. At the end of the night when you're laying in bed, maybe you just want someone that you can really open up to.

It's not just about sex, and it shouldn't ever be. That's certainly a great part of dating in general, but not what you should be seeking out. There are other ways to do that. You should be looking for a boyfriend, a husband, a lover, a *best friend*. Remember to stay true to that idea throughout this entire process. If you lose sight of your goal, you'll end up right where you started before you began reading this book. Never forget that at the end of the day, you're doing this for YOU.

Never Lose Yourself

You're the most important person in this entire process! If you lose yourself, or become someone completely different, what's the point? You might meet someone that you feel the need to change for. Maybe things are great at first and you just start pretending to like things you don't really care about in order to keep the peace. It might be good at first, but you never want to get in a committed relationship with someone that you have to change for. You'll never truly feel fulfilled if you allow yourself to become a different person.

If someone makes you compromise a part of you for them, they're not meant for you either. This can be a challenging thing to remember. Maybe you've been single for so long that you're desperate to keep someone around that really likes you. If you're not being authentic, however, then they still don't truly like *you*. Remember, it's better to be yourself and alone than to be living a lie with someone else.

If you let yourself become someone else and stay in a fake relationship, you'll find that you eventually become lonelier than if you never would have met anyone in the first place. True love is finding someone that you can be completely yourself with. You shouldn't have to fear what might happen if you stay true to who you are while dating another person.

Conclusion

Becoming more self-aware is one of the most important steps when starting the dating process. You are wired to be an emotional being. Your emotions are naturally ingrained into your brain to help protect you from various aspects of life. If you can learn to identify and control your emotions, you'll be surprised at just how far they can take you. Don't let your emotions dictate. It's perfectly fine to feel the way you feel, but the key is how you let your feelings control your actions. The most important thing for you to do is to take charge. You're in control! Emotions are not easy. This is probably going to be one of the most challenging things you'll have to face, but it's going to be one of the most important. Once you can do that, you can really build your confidence.

Improving your self-worth and self-esteem will help in every aspect in your life, not just your dating one. We've been taught for far too long that we're not valuable, pretty enough, skinny enough, funny enough, cool enough, and the list goes on and on. You have to always challenge these thoughts whenever you might have them and know that none of that is true! Don't say anything to yourself that you wouldn't say to an innocent person, someone like your little sibling, cousin, or even your pet. You don't deserve to be spoken down to, and that includes by yourself.

Set realistic expectations for the partner you want to find. You're not going to find someone that meets every point of your checklist. Even if you do, this might not be the person that you actually want to end up with. It's great to create a list of what you want in a partner and relationship, but you can't be too strict with that list. If you keep your vision too strict, you're going to let other things pass by that you didn't even know you needed.

Remember that you have to be attractive yourself in order to get a partner. Yes, you should always be yourself and stay true to who you are. That's something that we emphasized plenty throughout the book. Remember, however, to be the *best version* of yourself.

Online dating is scary, but it's necessary in our current world. There are plenty of people who have rejected the internet and all it has to offer, but it's a great tool to help you meet people that you wouldn't normally otherwise. There are still plenty of ways to meet people other than the internet, but don't shut this out as an option. You're going to run into some challenges when dating online, but that's inevitable. However, if you push through all the challenges you face, you just might end up meeting the love of your life.

Once you actually make it through the entire process, you can't forget how to actually maintain a healthy relationship with your partner. That's what you've worked so hard for! Remember that no time spent with anyone is a waste of time. If you've been with someone for half a decade, have a house together and maybe even a child, that doesn't mean you have to be with them forever if it isn't right. You're not obligated to make anyone happy but yourself, and you need to be sure you've entered in an equal partnership. That doesn't mean that you both have to contribute equal parts in everything you do, but just that finding the right balance for you both is the most important.

It's not going to be easy, but it's going to be the greatest thing you've ever felt. Think of the last ten songs you heard, or even the last movie you watched. There was a romance in it, right? Maybe the last song you listened to was about heartbreak, but romance was still involved. Romance novels are among the most popular books you can buy, and even the most action-packed or suspenseful TV show likely has a romantic plotline. Love is what makes the world go around. It's what keeps us getting out of bed in the morning and helps us power through our worst days. Of course, you don't need love, and loving yourself is just as important as loving your partner. If you manage to be one of the lucky ones to find love, you'll realize it's one of the greatest joys in your life. We believe that if you live true to the things we discussed in the book, you're going to find that happiness.

The most important thing to remember in this crazy process is to have fun. You're going to have moments when you want to give up. You'll likely shed some tears, maybe before you even get started. There's a chance that you might end up with a broken heart or be forced to hurt someone else (emotionally). It's not always going to be easy, but you still need to make sure that you're having fun. This shouldn't be work, and you shouldn't be torturing yourself in the process. Don't seek out a husband, look for your best friend. If someone doesn't like you or a date doesn't work out, don't blame yourself. You're going to want to do that right away, asking yourself over and over what you could have done differently. Not everyone is meant to be together, and that's OK.

One day, you're going to wake up on a weekend morning with no alarms set. The sun will be shining through the window onto you and your lover lying in bed. There's going to be a moment that they're still sleeping, and you take the chance to study their face. Watching someone you love sleep so peacefully is one of the greatest things you'll ever experience. When you make it to this moment, when you can look at someone and feel nothing but pure joy, you'll realize that everything you went through to get there was all worth it in the end.

www.ingramcontent.com/pod-product-compliance
Lightning Source LLC
Chambersburg PA
CBHW071006080526
44587CB00015B/2364